FINANCIAL VIBRATION

FINANCIAL VIBRATION

FINANCIAL VIBRATION

FINANCIAL VIBRATION

FINANCIAL VIBRATION

INDEX

LET US BEGIN...

Frequency of wealth

What is financial abundance?

Frequency of Wealth and Benefits

Attracting Compatible Patterns

Understand your vibratory buzz

What is Vibrational Balance?

Changing Your Vibration

Creating what you want

Learn the difference between desire and detachment

The Benefits of Planning for Financial Abundance

FINANCIAL VIBRATION

FINANCIAL VIBRATION

LET US BEGIN...

This book is designed to help you achieve financial prosperity by taking advantage of your internal resources that you may not know you have. You will learn that by shifting your vibrations and emotional frequencies from the negative to the positive, you will be able to stay focused and influence others to make success easier and with less effort.

FINANCIAL VIBRATION

Frequency of wealth

Do you think there are such things as vibrations or frequencies of wealth? Today, being prosperous or generally achieving what one wants in life seems to involve not only having the right resources, determination and skills. Possessing the right brain waves is also important; perhaps even the most important of all.

What is Wealth Frequency?

Studies suggest that meditation reduces brain waves to a lower frequency that is best for relaxing and focusing. This is known as low alpha. You can also lower your brain waves to reach the Theta frequency, which is best for lucid manifesting or dreaming. However, to tune in to the frequency of wealth, experts recommend raising brain waves.

Emotional Frequencies

In his book, Power vs. Force, David measured the frequencies of human emotions from 20 to 1,000. Hawkins suggests that at lower frequencies, people are solid or heavy while they are light and bright at higher frequencies where we get feelings of peace, love, acceptance and other positive feelings that allow us to better understand and see more clearly.

Hawkins proposes that when you are at lower frequencies, for example 20 (shame), 30

FINANCIAL VIBRATION

(guilt), 75 (grief), 100 (fear) and 175 (pain), (pride), you are more prone to illnesses and problems because these emotions are running out and you are likely to extend more guilt, more fear, etc..., emotions that drag you and others you come in contact with.

When you are at higher frequency levels, you are able to influence others in a more positive way. To support this concept, the Global

The Princeton Consciousness Project detected a negative consciousness just before the attack on the Twin Towers on September 21, 2001. On the other hand, it detected a positive blip prior to President Barack Obama's inauguration, demonstrating that individuals are affected by the frequencies as a whole and that the earth is affected by the combined energies of individuals.

Changing thought patterns

Raising brain waves does not necessarily raise your frequency but it changes your thought patterns and you need to do this if you want to successfully diminish the effects of your ego on your decision-making and your dealings with others.

How then can you find your frequency for wealth? Well, obviously the first step is to adjust your thought patterns to one that allows you to think more objectively and clearly. The second is that you try to get up from the emotional frequencies that hold you back.

FINANCIAL VIBRATION

Acceptance, peace, love, goodwill, courage; all these emotions are positive and belong to the higher frequencies that allow them to influence others more positively.

According to a related study, an individual who operates at 300 is able to counter 90,000 people who operate below 200 levels, while an individual who operates at 600 (peace) is able to counter 10,000,000 people who operate below 200.

The ability to influence others is the key to finding the frequency of their wealth. This does not mean that you will not experience any failure, but as you are clear-minded, focused and in contact with a higher level of consciousness, wealth is much easier to achieve than when you are operating at the frequency levels of energy drainage.

FINANCIAL VIBRATION

What is financial abundance?

The life you have always dreamed of can be achieved through proper mentality and actions. If you want to be free of any financial worries, then achieve financial abundance. What it is and what it can do to your life is incredible. So, here are the things you should know about financial abundance.

Financial abundance is being in a situation where there is enough financial support to sustain your life and add a few more for your convenience.

It is far from financial burdens and worries

FINANCIAL VIBRATION

and there is a feeling of having enough abundance where stress and pressure do not get in the way. To achieve financial abundance, you can follow these essential factors:

What is financial abundance?

1. Learn to Strengthen Your Mind

Learn to practice a mentality full of abundance. With this, learn that money is only a material thing and should not be the source of satisfaction. Of course, who does not need money? This abundant mentality is different in such a way that it must be practiced to balance your life. Do not allow greed to overcome you. Instead, enjoy your money by saving a little and giving it away to help. With that, your motive becomes so positive and this will eventually align with your goals. This is what is called getting positive vibrations.

2. Gain knowledge

This is not limited to the academic level. In fact, many rich people have less knowledge than the poor. This knowledge means adapting what you have learned (from school or personal experience) and finding ways to use it. This knowledge will translate into your ability, where your ability can give you financial abundance. Living a life you are passionate about counts for a life of abundance. With this, you can earn money eventually.

3. The Art of Generosity

When you want something in your life, help other people achieve their dreams too. There have been many sayings about generosity and one that is true is that we get back what we give. This does not mean that generosity means donating money. Yes, it can be done, but it doesn't all count in money, does it? So in order for you to achieve a comfortable and abundant life, create a positive environment to get what you want. Now, this vindicates the old saying: it's better to give than to receive.

4. The Way to Invest

Don't keep too much of your money. In fact, saving it doesn't necessarily mean you're creating an abundant life. Yes, saving for emergencies and unexpected expenses is important, but it shouldn't be a way to ease your financial burden. What you have to do is invest. Invest in something that will give you a significant return in a specific time period. With that, there is a great chance that you can earn more income apart from your job.

FINANCIAL VIBRATION

Frequency of Wealth and Benefits

The Law of Vibration

The law of vibration establishes that everything that exists in the universe is nothing more than an energy that vibrates at different frequencies. Whether physical matter or the invisible (spirit, chi, etc.), everything vibrates to a certain pulse.

Following that paradigm, everything that exists is in the continuum of energies and frequencies. One part is the frequency of wealth.

FINANCIAL VIBRATION

By being able to touch and resonate with that tone, you can create more of that condition in your life.

David Hawkins Calibration David Hawkins came with the calibration of human energies and emotions starting at 20-1000 frequencies. The lower frequencies are dense, states like guilt (30), hatred, sadness; love and peace are in the range of 500 to 600.

The first positive state of emotion is calibrated from 200 (value) and above. To reach the situations and the tiny components consisting of the idea of "wealth", these individual pieces must be made to resonate from the age of 200.

Calibration is not important; this is just a guide, a number we can use to calibrate up or down the spectrum of emotions or human states to achieve the effects we want.

Law of Resonance and Attraction

The law of resonance and attraction are similar but not identical ideas. Because there are different types of wealth concepts and ideas, wealth that resonates generically will attract those situations that cause financial abundance.

The law of resonance creates the distinction of whether you will attract more of one thing over another. An example is the law of resonance which differentiates whether the chair or a table can be manifested, although both are in the universal category called furniture.

Frequency Broadcasting with Deliberate Wealth

By training your mind to live on this frequency and charging it with intensity and resonance, teaching the same to everyone in your environment, i.e. employees, business partners, and even charging the physical space in which you are, you are increasing the likelihood of attracting favorable conditions to wealth.

Initially, it may take a lot of conscious effort to enter that headspace because that is not how we usually think, feel and see the world. With the passage of time, you will feel more organic and the time will come when it will become your frequency or base state.

The Midas touch

Once you become naturally resonant at this frequency, the phenomenon of the "Midas touch" begins to manifest in your life. Everything you touch seems to work effortlessly and naturally on its own, doing nothing consciously.

That is an explanation of why success begets success. It creates the impetus for success where success opens the doors for future success and so on.

FINANCIAL VIBRATION

The metaphor of the immune system

Anyone who has achieved the highest levels of success has naturally trained to think and operate on these frequencies. Things that don't happen as planned are unnatural and are eliminated, like the immune system that kills invaders.

Diseases are negativities, and positive frequencies (for wealth) are the immune system's super-soldiers of antibodies that defend themselves automatically and naturally.

FINANCIAL VIBRATION

Attracting Compatible Patterns

Everything in the universe is just energy, and if you look deep enough, you will see that everything is just vibrations and that these vibratory patterns are what turn gas into gases and liquids and solids into what they are. This includes intangibles such as spirit and soul. It can be helpful to see the states of matter beginning with the ether, the spirit/soul, the gases, the liquids and finally the solids.

This does not mean that you can physically move heavy objects with your mind alone, although some claim to be able to do so through telekinesis.

That is beyond the scope of this book.

The goal of manifestation through the attraction of compatible energy patterns is to create a path of least resistance by which manifestation is possible and is a better path than the opposite of what we want.

An explanation of luck and bad luck

"If you create within yourself and without the conditions in which an event is easier to engender, something that we would consider "luck", such luck would have to be easier to manifest in an environment full of negativity and forces that say the opposite, conditions that include "bad luck".

Due to the recent popularity of The Secret, many have misunderstood the idea of being just illusions and not taking action. Action is also energy. It is a component of force, a physical force that makes use of intangible energy and vibrations created to make things happen in the real world.

Practical aspects of energy use in the real world

There is only the attraction of ideal situations, people and events. The power of these effects generated through this channel exists in the more subtle and intangible realms, unlike physical actions that are stronger. It is not realistic to physically move an object that

FINANCIAL VIBRATION

weighs a ton by these means. This requires mechanical energy, tools and devices such as a crane.

And how does a crane manifest itself?

You can call the company that leases large industrial machinery. You can establish contacts and make friends within the heavy machinery industry. You can visualize intensely, act as if you already have the crane. It's not just about using one on top of the other; it's about applying as many working methods as possible to achieve that goal.

On your own, I doubt that you can manifest a crane only with your mind, much less with an object that weighs a ton to levitate to another place. It's just not realistic and based on fantasy!

Creating Compatible Patterns for Wealth and

Abundance

The above example speaks of a very specific objective that can be solved by mechanical means, i.e. a crane. However, to design a general living condition with many possible variables, approach paths and results, we cannot simply reduce a problem to a single thing like a crane. And this is where hitting the law of attraction, attracts what attracts what attracts what can be useful.

By creating the right vibrations and energies within ourselves and our businesses, we are able to attract coincidences, people and resources that would not normally fall into our laps without seemingly good luck. Because we have created the right energy signatures to make these variables not only attracted but residing congruently in our space.

In short, it is about creating the right energies to magnetize assets and create a sustainable framework in which assets and resources can be maintained organically in our space or sphere of influence where these things are useful. Although they exist in the realm of intangibles, and cannot be measured with our earthly scientific devices, there is nothing to lose by taking advantage of this reserve of power available to all of us!

FINANCIAL VIBRATION

Understand your vibratory buzz

Everything creates vibrations, subtle and perceptible only for those who seek them. Knowing and understanding vibrations, including one's own, is very important for living a prosperous and abundant life. There are two types of vibrations or energy: positive and negative. The positive energy you already know allows you to influence others and therefore do more, and the negative energy drags you down along with those around you.

Once you have learned to identify vibrations or energy as others call them, be sure to stick only to the positive ones, as this will help you elevate your own. Avoid negative vibrations that can lower or diminish theirs.

The first step you need to take so that you can benefit from the power of the vibrations that are continually released into the environment is to learn to detect and classify them. There is a proven method of doing this. Think of the vibrations you feel when a train runs on its tracks. There may not be a real train running, but you know the vibrations it produces.

Relax and open your senses to what surrounds you and you will be able to feel them. It will take time, but eventually, and with patience, you will learn to notice them. Doing meditations that erase the ordinary noises of everyday life helps. With time, you will even be able to see them by keeping your eyes out of focus while you are meditating. You must acquire the ability to notice the vibrations if you want to benefit from their powers.

Knowing your own vibrations

The next step, after you have acquired the ability to feel and see vibrations, is to divert your attention to yourself. This will require some time for deep analysis and reflection on what your present is. You will know what they are by the attitudes you have about certain things that are of general importance to people and to yourself.

You just need to be honest with yourself.

It is important to know your vibratory buzz as it has a direct effect on how you live your life. It would be very difficult for you to achieve your goals in life if you don't know where you currently are.

Raising Your Vibrations

After identifying where you are regarding your buzzing vibrations, the next step you take is to try to raise your vibrations. There are numerous ways to accomplish this and the more you apply it, the easier it is for you to prosper and live an abundant life. One of the ways that has proven effective in raising vibrations is to maintain good health. Eating

FINANCIAL VIBRATION

healthier foods, drinking lots of water and avoiding toxin-laden foods raises your vibrations. Meditation, learning to relax and develop the right attitudes, focusing more on the passions of your life will also greatly help to improve your vibrations.

Generally, the happier you are, the more positive your vibrations are.

You can raise your vibrations to even higher levels by associating only with people with positive vibrations.

FINANCIAL VIBRATION

What is Vibrational Balance?

Because you're a vibrating being, you send signals that tell others who you are. Not everyone receives your signals, of course, but those whose signals are aligned with yours.

If you are sending happy signals, others who are equally happy will pick up their signals and there will be two-way communication. This is how vibratory beings communicate in a vibratory world. It is called attracting compatible patterns. This promotes harmony.

FINANCIAL VIBRATION

Attracting Compatible Patterns

If you recognize yourself as a vibrating being, you want to attract the signals that would benefit you. Before you can do that, you must understand your vibratory buzz. How? You turn inward. This can be done by simply calming your mind, blocking distracting noises and listening to the signals you are releasing.

Do you feel happy, sad, frustrated, depressed or contented? Your vibrations or signals will reflect whatever feeling you have, and you will receive the same vibrations from your surroundings.

FINANCIAL VIBRATION

Vibrational Balance

As a vibrating being, your world is governed by signals that you release and receive. In time, you will reach vibratory balance, which is characterized by the dominant signal you send and receive.

Compatibility provides stability, but is that the kind of stability you would like? For example, if you have been living under financial stress for years and this has ceased to cause you discouragement of frustration, it could only mean that your vibratory balance is in tune with this kind of life.

The only way to change a vibratory balance

that prevents you from doing more things like becoming more prosperous is to change your vibration.

Changing Your Vibrational Balance

Achieving a permanent change in vibrations is not easy. This cannot be achieved, for example, by changing clothes, showering or exercising.

Whatever good feelings you get from doing these things can alter your vibrations; but only temporarily.

To change your vibratory balance, your efforts should focus on changing the dominant signals you release. A permanent disconnection from the environment that supports your negative balance must be your priority or you will continue to return to your previous state.

There are two methods to switch from your current negative balance to one that is more empowering. The first is to change your signals in a way that allows you to repel the signals from your surroundings.

You can focus your mind and energies on your goals and this new focus that is incompatible with your current environment will slowly change that environment as you will be attracting new signals. You will be seeing and experiencing new things and eventually your physical reality will be aligned with your new vibrations.

FINANCIAL VIBRATION

An effective technique to prevent your environment from interfering with your efforts to change vibrations is to graphically visualize your goals for at least 20 minutes a day. Put strong emotions into it and gradually you will notice that the signals you will pick up are the ones that reinforce your vibrations.

Another approach is to move physically or socially away from your current environment. You can do this by moving to a place where the signals are different or you can stop seeing lazy and carefree friends.

Once you have changed the vibrations, your vibratory balance will change.

FINANCIAL VIBRATION

Changing Your Vibration

Your mind is more powerful than it can really conspire with the universe.

What we say, think and feel creates an invisible vibration that transmits energy.

This energy now conspires with what we call quantum space where everything is unlimited and anyone can be given opportunities. That is why it is also considered an energetic being; not only because of physical factors, but also because it can receive and transmit energy. Do you want to be successful in life? Then learn to change your vibration.

FINANCIAL VIBRATION

It's not about what you want. What you think, feel and dream about in life can attract vibrations to it, but that doesn't necessarily mean that you will get it. These are just parts of it and what matters most is how you are pointing to the universe to get what you want. You create vibrations as you continue to exchange energy; so there will come a time when uncontrollable circumstances occur that cause the signal to be interrupted. With that, you need to harmonize everything in your life with what you want to do and repel those who stand in your way.

Therefore, if a certain situation makes you feel frustrated, angry, or unmotivated, it reflects a negative signal. Combat it by being surrounded by positive people and give energy that will make you feel good despite the circumstances.

FINANCIAL VIBRATION

The Need to Feel Your Vibration

Stay in touch with yourself as you practice a way to create an inner peace. To cool the good vibrations, keep a calm mind and listen to your body. This can be in the form of prayer or meditation - whatever you call it is fine. You just need to eliminate any thoughts and concentrate on being quiet and at peace.

You can take a long walk on the beach or just take a vacation away from the city. For practical reasons, you can even have a good silence or time for yourself in your own room. As you stay quiet, let your emotions in. Feel anything, shout it out if you can and get it all out of your system. Feel your body's signals. There may be times when you feel a

FINANCIAL VIBRATION

mixture of emotions, as you may be completely sad and eventually feel comfort and peace. There are times when you are so happy and vibrant. Feel them and feel your vibration.

The Change of Vibration

Now that you are equipped to know how vibrations react to your mind, and how you can feel them, you can change your vibration toward your goal. The first thing you can do is disconnect yourself from the environment that interrupts your signal. Don't have negative thoughts or even negative people. Here's a practical tip: visualize your goal every day for 15 minutes.

Feel your emotions so strong and eventually,

FINANCIAL VIBRATION

you can listen to your vibrations and know how to repel the things that will block your path. The next thing you can do is change your environment. You can go out with people with strong goals like yours, change the style of your house or even change the way you dress. All of this should make you feel good and create a strong vibration.

Creating what you want

At this point in this book, you should know that if you want a more rewarding life, you have to change your way of thinking, and your whole way of thinking. Here are some more tips on how you can create what you want and get what you want:

Tips & Tricks:

Tip 1: Keep your focus where it matters

Don't think about what you don't have, because if you do, you'll never have enough. This is very fundamental advice that once taken into account, will significantly influence your life in a positive way.

Changing your focus and what you focus on will radically change your life.

If you concentrate on what you don't have, your mind and soul will continue to think you are missing something. On the other hand, when you make a regular habit of being grateful for what you DO have, you will be able to train the positive energies around you to give yourself what you want.

With this kind of mentality, you will be able to easily find solutions to common and not so common problems in your life. You will be more open to positive responses and opportunities around you, making winning easier.

Tip 2: Define Failure Differently

One of the things that limit people from achieving great things is their fear of failure. We all feel this at a certain time in our lives. We are afraid to fail and to suffer the consequences of failure.

However, once you define failure in a more positive way, things will change drastically for you, including your perspective on failure.

Don't believe in failure. Instead, define failure as an opportunity to learn, to be better at what you just did. Without failure, we would never be who we are, and who we are. So instead of seeing failure as something bigger than you that scares you, look at it as a ladder to your goals. Teach your mind to redefine failure, from being a negative thing that drags, to a positive and uplifting opportunity to become a more complete person.

Tip 3: You Are the Teacher of Yourself

Who's your boss? No one else should be your boss but YOU. It all depends on you what you want to happen to your life. There is no one more responsible for you than YOU. By recognizing and accepting the fact that there is no one else who can help you build your successful future, you will become more mature and inspired to do better things for yourself.

FINANCIAL VIBRATION

Harnessing the power of the universe and making it believe what you want for yourself will be easy from now on. As you practice these tips every day, you will be more attentive to the positive things that affect the successful people around you. Then you will be able to harness this power, and make it happen for you.

FINANCIAL VIBRATION

Learn the difference between desire and detachment

Many people, armed with the best intentions and skills, still don't get what they want simply because of their misconceptions about these two things: desire and detachment.

The first thing you should know about the two is that they are not opposites to each other. However, they are intertwined because they can make the Law of Attractions work in their favor or not.

FINANCIAL VIBRATION

Most people think of this as a state synonymous with wanting or needing something. However, when it comes to the Law of Attractions, desire is more than that. In fact, the best way to appreciate how important desire is in a person's life is to see it as the result of having personal preferences.

What is desire?

Knowing what you don't prefer in your life can help you find out what you want in it. As such, knowing that you don't like sour food can lead you to discover that you like sweets or perhaps spicy food. These preferences can be seen as desires. In other words, you simply want to eat spicy food instead of sour dishes.

Desire is also often mistakenly considered immoral. Some people see desire as "bad" because it can lead to greed, selfishness, envy, and many other negative emotions. However, that is where they are wrong once again.

Consider the above example. Is it sinful, immoral, or wrong if you want spicy food instead of sour food?

In addition, there are many desires that one could hardly describe as erroneous or, even worse, evil. Some people just want to be healthy. Others may want to be able to help those in need.

Detachment

However, desire can be counterproductive and become its undoing when accompanied by feelings of attachment... or detachment.

- Attachment - Your desire is exceptionally strong, to the point that you feel negative emotions because of it. You feel pressured about your ability to achieve your goal. You are worried and afraid of the consequences if you don't get what you want.

- Disinterest - Desire is the only thing that worries you. You don't feel anything else. You are unable to empathize or sympathize with the feelings of others because everything in you is completely focused on getting what you want.

Consider, for example, a student with a desire to get good grades.

Feelings of attachment can cause the student to worry endlessly about the results of tests that begin to suffer from nervous attacks and insomnia. On the other hand, a student with the same desire may use detachment as a coping mechanism. In this case, the student spends his or her time studying to the point of excluding everything else, such as eating and sleeping regularly or treating loved ones with indifference.

Desire and detachment are obviously two different things, but they can be experienced at the same time. Ultimately, it is the non-attachment to which you must aspire if you wish your desires to be fulfilled.

The feelings of non-attachment free you from negative thoughts and emotions and at the same time motivate you to do and think better in order to achieve your goal.

FINANCIAL VIBRATION

The Benefits of Planning for Financial Abundance

At this time, some of you may feel convinced that you know all there is to do to have the best attitude and mentality to enjoy financial abundance. That's fine, but you have to keep in mind that financial abundance also requires smart, strategic, practical and tangible actions. That's when the planning stage comes in.

6 Key Steps to Creating a Financial Abundance Plan

Planning is a process that takes time to create, complete and refine. Take your time to come up with the best plan. Changes will be more difficult and more costly to implement if you make them after the plans have been finalized.

Step 1: Increase Cash Flow

The first goal your plan should focus on is to increase your cash flow. It may not mean more profit, income or sales, but it does mean more financial flexibility. Another way to increase your cash flow is to simply reduce costs. With more cash on hand, you also give yourself better leverage to solve the problem, sudden financial crises and take advantage of opportunities to earn money.

Step 2: Investing in Health and Insurance

Health problems are one of the biggest sources of spending, so be sure to save yourself from future headaches by investing in health plans and insurance now. Speaking of insurance, it's also best to insure most - or best of all - that you have that is valuable and worth protecting. Consider investing in life insurance that also has a reasonably good payment.

Step 3: Debt Management and Elimination

It's time to stop delaying the inevitable. Today, debts are rarely repaid. Most of the time, there's no way out of them, so it's best to buckle up and find out which debts are the most pressing and which deserve another round of negotiation with their respective creditors. Of course, this does not mean that debt is always a bad thing.

Debt can mean higher cash inflows and the possibility of allowing for infrequent investment opportunities. Just be sure to borrow only what you need or at least what you can afford.

Step 4: Increase Savings

This certainly doesn't need any further explanation. Savings are probably the safest way to safeguard your retirement and your future in general. Just keep in mind that savings can come in many forms; so choose wisely!

Step 5: Investments

Passive income is always essential in any plan to achieve financial abundance. Investments are certainly one of the most lucrative sources of passive income, but they can also be one of the most risky. Be sure to tread carefully when choosing the investment you will trust with your hard-earned money.

Step 6: Estate Planning

Finally, it's never too late to start planning what will happen to your estate if for some reason you're unable to manage it.

Writing your own will and making sure it's

FINANCIAL VIBRATION

airtight and legal is something you can do on your own, of course, but only if you're willing to take the time to study all the details of estate planning.

The above steps are clearly easier said than done, but they will pave the way to financial abundance if you commit to your own plan.

Visit our author page on Amazon and get more MENTES LIBRES!

http://amazon.com/author/menteslibres

If you wish, you can leave a comment on this book by clicking on the following link so that we can continue to grow! Thank you very much for your purchase!

https://www.amazon.com/dp/B082FPPNLB

www.ingramcontent.com/pod-product-compliance
Lightning Source LLC
Chambersburg PA
CBHW070826220526
45466CB00002B/765